MW00478857

In case of loss, please return to:

_____

_____

_____

Hello! Welcome to your new travel journal.
Hopefully this will be your new companion
for many adventures to come.

Here's how to use this journal:

Place to attach things!
(Try using a glue stick)

A quote to inspire your story-telling!

The world is a book, and those who do not travel read only a page.
- Saint Augustine

ADMIT ONE

ADMIT ONE

Plenty of space on each page to write!

Safe travels!

*Attach photos, ticket stubs,
other souvenirs or sketches*

Begin to look at maps with the narcotic tingle of possibility.
— Rolf Potts

Date:

*Attach photos, ticket stubs,
other souvenirs or sketches*

My favorite thing to do is go where I've never been.
— Diane Arbus

Date:

Attach photos, ticket stubs,
other souvenirs or sketches

It's a big world out there. It would be a shame not to experience it.
— JD Andrews

Date: _____

Attach photos, ticket stubs,
other souvenirs or sketches

Too often I would hear men boast of the miles covered that day,
rarely of what they had seen. — Louis L'Amour

Date:

Attach photos, ticket stubs,
other souvenirs or sketches

Courage is the power to let go of the familiar.
— Raymond Lindquist

Date:

_____

_____
_____
_____
_____
_____
_____
_____
_____
_____
_____
_____
_____
_____
_____
_____
_____
_____
_____
_____
_____
_____
_____
_____
_____
_____
_____
_____
_____
_____

Attach photos, ticket stubs,
other souvenirs or sketches

He who must travel happily must travel light.
— Antione de Saint-Exupery

Date:

*Attach photos, ticket stubs,
other souvenirs or sketches*

I haven't been everywhere, but it's on my list.
— Susan Sontag

Date:

_____
_____
_____
_____
_____
_____
_____
_____
_____
_____
_____
_____
_____
_____
_____
_____
_____
_____
_____
_____
_____
_____
_____
_____
_____
_____
_____
_____
_____
_____
_____

Attach photos, ticket stubs,
other souvenirs or sketches

I just wish the world was twice as big and half of it was still unexplored. — David Attenborough

Date:

Attach photos, ticket stubs,
other souvenirs or sketches

A good traveler has no fixed plans and is not intent on arriving.
— Lao Tzu

Date:

*Attach photos, ticket stubs,
other souvenirs or sketches*

I travel for travel's sake. The great affair is to move.
— Robert Louis Stevenson

Date:

*Attach photos, ticket stubs,
other souvenirs or sketches*

A journey is best measured in friends, rather than miles.
— Tim Cahill

Date:

Attach photos, ticket stubs,
other souvenirs or sketches

Not all those who wander are lost.
— J.R.R. Tolkien

Date:

*Attach photos, ticket stubs,
other souvenirs or sketches*

Stop worrying about the potholes in the road and celebrate the journey. — Barbara Hoffman

Date:

Attach photos, ticket stubs,
other souvenirs or sketches

All journeys have secret destinations of which the traveler is unaware. — Martin Buber

Date:

Attach photos, ticket stubs,
other souvenirs or sketches

Make voyages. Attempt them — there's nothing else.
— Tennessee Williams

Date:

Attach photos, ticket stubs, other souvenirs or sketches

Once a year, go someplace you've never been before.
— Dalai Lama

Date:

_____

_____

_____

_____

_____

_____

_____

_____

_____

_____

_____

_____

_____

_____

_____

_____

_____

_____

_____

_____

_____

_____

_____

_____

_____

_____

_____

_____

*Attach photos, ticket stubs,
other souvenirs or sketches*

To travel is to discover that everyone else is wrong about other countries. — Aldous Huxley

Date:

*Attach photos, ticket stubs,
other souvenirs or sketches*

The real voyage of discovery comes not in seeking new landscapes, but in having new eyes. — Marcel Proust

Date:

Attach photos, ticket stubs,
other souvenirs or sketches

The more I traveled, the more I realized that fear makes strangers of people who should be friends. — Shirley MacLaine

Date:

*Attach photos, ticket stubs,
other souvenirs or sketches*

Once the travel bug bites, these is no antidote and I know that I shall be happily infected until the end of my life. — Michael Palin

Date:
_____

_____
_____
_____
_____
_____
_____
_____
_____
_____
_____
_____
_____
_____
_____
_____
_____
_____
_____
_____
_____
_____
_____
_____
_____
_____
_____
_____
_____
_____
_____
_____
_____
_____
_____
_____
_____

Attach photos, ticket stubs,
other souvenirs or sketches

Better to see something once than to hear about it a thousand times.
— Asian Proverb

Date:

Attach photos, ticket stubs,
other souvenirs or sketches

The impulse to travel is one of the hopeful symptoms of life.
— Agnes Repplier

Date:

*Attach photos, ticket stubs,
other souvenirs or sketches*

Traveling is still the most intense form of learning.
— Kevin Kelly

Date:

Attach photos, ticket stubs, other souvenirs or sketches

Travel far enough you meet yourself.
— David Mitchell

Date: _____

Attach photos, ticket stubs,
other souvenirs or sketches

Since life is short and the world is wide, the sooner you start exploring it, the better. — Eckhart Tolle

Date:

Attach photos, ticket stubs,
other souvenirs or sketches

I am not the same for having seen the moon shine on the other side of the world. — Mary Anne Radmacher

Date:

Attach photos, ticket stubs,
other souvenirs or sketches

The best journeys are those which answer questions you never thought to ask. — Rick Ridgeway

Date:

Attach photos, ticket stubs,
other souvenirs or sketches

Above all, watch with glittering eyes the whole world around you.
— Roald Dahl

Date:

Attach photos, ticket stubs,
other souvenirs or sketches

Traveling. It leaves you speechless, then it turns you into a storyteller. — Ibn Battuta

Date:

*Attach photos, ticket stubs,
other souvenirs or sketches*

Travel brings power and love back to your life.
— Rumi

Date:
_____

_____
_____
_____
_____
_____
_____
_____
_____
_____
_____
_____
_____
_____
_____
_____
_____
_____
_____
_____
_____
_____
_____
_____
_____
_____
_____
_____

Attach photos, ticket stubs,
other souvenirs or sketches

It's good to have an end to journey toward, but it's the journey that matters in the end. — Ernest Hemingway

Date:

Attach photos, ticket stubs, other souvenirs or sketches

Wherever you go, go with all your heart.
— Confucius

Date:

*Attach photos, ticket stubs,
other souvenirs or sketches*

The gladdest moment in human life, methinks, is a departure into unknown lands. — Sir Richard Burton

Date:

*Attach photos, ticket stubs,
other souvenirs or sketches*

Travel makes one modest. You see what a tiny place you occupy in the world. — Gustave Flaubert

Date:

_____
_____
_____
_____
_____
_____
_____
_____
_____
_____
_____
_____
_____
_____
_____
_____
_____
_____
_____
_____
_____
_____
_____
_____
_____
_____
_____
_____
_____
_____
_____
_____

*Attach photos, ticket stubs,
other souvenirs or sketches*

We travel not to escape life, but for life not to escape us.
— Anonymous

Date:

Attach photos, ticket stubs,
other souvenirs or sketches

You don't have to be rich to travel well.
— Eugene Fodor

Date:

*Attach photos, ticket stubs,
other souvenirs or sketches*

I travel a lot; I hate having my life disrupted by routine.
— Caskie Stinnett

Date:

_____

_____

_____

_____

_____

_____

_____

_____

_____

_____

_____

_____

_____

_____

_____

_____

_____

_____

_____

_____

_____

_____

_____

_____

_____

_____

_____

_____

Attach photos, ticket stubs,
other souvenirs or sketches

Travel is fatal to prejudice, bigotry, and narrow-mindedness.
— Mark Twain

Date:

Attach photos, ticket stubs,
other souvenirs or sketches

He who does not travel does not know the value of men.
— Moorish proverb

Date:

Attach photos, ticket stubs,
other souvenirs or sketches

A traveler without observation is a bird without wings.
— Moslih Eddin Saadi

Date:

Attach photos, ticket stubs,
other souvenirs or sketches

Travel is more than the seeing of sights. It is a change that goes on deep and permanent in the minds of the living. — Miriam Beard

Date:

*Attach photos, ticket stubs,
other souvenirs or sketches*

Tourists don't know where they've been. Travelers don't know where they're going. — Paul Theroux

Date:

Attach photos, ticket stubs,
other souvenirs or sketches

A journey of a thousand miles begins with a single step.
— Lao Tzu

Date:

Attach photos, ticket stubs,
other souvenirs or sketches

There is no moment of delight in any pilgrimage like the
beginning of it. — Charles Dudley Warner

Date:

*Attach photos, ticket stubs,
other souvenirs or sketches*

The journey not the arrival matters.
— T. S. Eliot

Date:

*Attach photos, ticket stubs,
other souvenirs or sketches*

To travel is to awaken.
— Lily Tsay

Date:

Attach photos, ticket stubs,
other souvenirs or sketches

A nomad I will remain for life, in love with distant and uncharted places. — Isabelle Eberhardt

Date:

Attach photos, ticket stubs,
other souvenirs or sketches

Somewhere, something incredible is waiting to be known.
— Carl Sagan

Date:

Attach photos, ticket stubs, other souvenirs or sketches

We travel, initially, to lose ourselves. And we travel, next, to find ourselves. — Anonymous

Date:

Attach photos, ticket stubs, other souvenirs or sketches

Getting lost is not a waste of time. To travel is to evolve.
— Pierre Bernard

Date:

Attach photos, ticket stubs, other souvenirs or sketches

The true fruit of travel is perhaps the feeling of being nearly everywhere at home. — Freya Stark

Date:

_____
_____
_____
_____
_____
_____
_____
_____
_____
_____
_____
_____
_____
_____
_____
_____
_____
_____
_____
_____
_____
_____
_____
_____
_____
_____
_____
_____
_____
_____
_____
_____

Attach photos, ticket stubs,
other souvenirs or sketches

I was not born for one corner. The whole world is my native land.
— Anonymous

Date:

_____

_____

_____

_____

_____

_____

_____

_____

_____

_____

_____

_____

_____

_____

_____

_____

_____

_____

_____

_____

_____

_____

_____

_____

_____

_____

_____

_____

_____

Attach photos, ticket stubs,
other souvenirs or sketches

If we were meant to stay in one place, we'd have roots instead of feet.
— Rachel Wolchin

Date:

Attach photos, ticket stubs,
other souvenirs or sketches

Be brave. Take risks. Nothing can substitute experience.
— Paulo Coelho

Date:

*Attach photos, ticket stubs,
other souvenirs or sketches*

Do not go where the path may lead. Go instead where there is no path and leave a trail. — Ralph Waldo Emerson

Date:

*Attach photos, ticket stubs,
other souvenirs or sketches*

There is a kind of magicness in going far away and then coming back all changed. — Kate Douglas Wiggin

Date:

Attach photos, ticket stubs,
other souvenirs or sketches

We take photos as a return ticket to a moment otherwise gone.
— Anonymous

Date:

Attach photos, ticket stubs,
other souvenirs or sketches

Travel teaches tolerance.
—Benjamin Disraeli

Date:

*Attach photos, ticket stubs,
other souvenirs or sketches*

A ship in harbor is safe, but that is not what ships are built for.
— John A. Shedd

Date:

Attach photos, ticket stubs, other souvenirs or sketches

Live, travel, adventure, bless, and don't be sorry.
— Jack Kerouac

Date:

Attach photos, ticket stubs, other souvenirs or sketches

The more places I travel to, the more I see, the more I learn, the less I know, and I love it! — Burt Robertson

Date:

Attach photos, ticket stubs,
other souvenirs or sketches

There is no end to the adventures we can have if only we seek them
with our eyes open. — Jawaharlal Nehru

Date:

Attach photos, ticket stubs,
other souvenirs or sketches

Travel is glamorous only in retrospect.
— Paul Theroux

Date:

Attach photos, ticket stubs,
other souvenirs or sketches

To travel is to take a journey into yourself.
— Danny Kaye

Date:

Attach photos, ticket stubs,
other souvenirs or sketches

People don't take trips. Trips take people.
— John Steinbeck

Date:

Attach photos, ticket stubs,
other souvenirs or sketches

Adventure is worthwhile.
— Aristotle

Date:

Attach photos, ticket stubs,
other souvenirs or sketches

If you think adventure is dangerous, try routine! It's lethal.
— Anonymous

Date:

Attach photos, ticket stubs, other souvenirs or sketches

Half the fun of travel is the esthetic of lostness.
— Ray Bradbury

Date:

Attach photos, ticket stubs,
other souvenirs or sketches

I see my path, but I don't know where it leads. Not knowing where I'm going is what inspires me to travel it. — Rosalia de Castro

Date:

Attach photos, ticket stubs, other souvenirs or sketches

If it scares you, it might be a good thing to try.
— Seth Godin

Date:

_____
_____
_____
_____
_____
_____
_____
_____
_____
_____
_____
_____
_____
_____
_____
_____
_____
_____
_____
_____
_____
_____
_____
_____
_____
_____
_____
_____
_____
_____
_____
_____
_____
_____

Attach photos, ticket stubs,
other souvenirs or sketches

Just to travel is rather boring, but to travel with a purpose is educational and exciting. — Sargent Shriver

Date:

Attach photos, ticket stubs,
other souvenirs or sketches

One doesn't discover new lands without consenting to lose sight of the shore for a very long time. — Andre Gide

Date:

Attach photos, ticket stubs,
other souvenirs or sketches

When you travel, remember that a foreign country is not designed to make you comfortable. — Clifton Faidman

Date:

Attach photos, ticket stubs,
other souvenirs or sketches

Adventures are the best way to learn.
— Anonymous

Date:

*Attach photos, ticket stubs,
other souvenirs or sketches*

Experience, travel — these are as education in themselves.
— Euripides

Date:

Attach photos, ticket stubs,
other souvenirs or sketches

One thing that I love about traveling is feeling disoriented and
removed from my comfort zone. — Sarah Glidden

Date:

*Attach photos, ticket stubs,
other souvenirs or sketches*

Throw off the bowlines. Sail away from the safe harbor.
Explore. Dream. Discover. — Mark Twain

Date:

*Attach photos, ticket stubs,
other souvenirs or sketches*

To awaken alone in a strange town is one of the pleasantest sensations in the world. — Freya Stark

Date:

_____
_____
_____
_____
_____
_____
_____
_____
_____
_____
_____
_____
_____
_____
_____
_____
_____
_____
_____
_____
_____
_____
_____
_____
_____
_____
_____
_____
_____
_____
_____
_____

Attach photos, ticket stubs, other souvenirs or sketches

Travel: the best way to be lost and found all at the same time.
— Brenna Smith

Date:

Attach photos, ticket stubs,
other souvenirs or sketches

Like all great travelers, I have seen more than I remember, and remember more than I have seen. — Benjamin Disraeli

Date:

*Attach photos, ticket stubs,
other souvenirs or sketches*

The first condition of understanding a foreign country is to smell it.
— Rudyard Kipling

Date:

Attach photos, ticket stubs, other souvenirs or sketches

Every perfect traveler always creates the country where he travels.
— Nikos Kazantzakis

Date:

Attach photos, ticket stubs, other souvenirs or sketches

The open road is a beckoning, a strangeness, a place where
a man can lose himself. — William Least Heat Moon

Date:

Attach photos, ticket stubs,
other souvenirs or sketches

Bizarre travel plans are dancing lessons from God.
— Kurt Vonnegut

Date:

Attach photos, ticket stubs, other souvenirs or sketches

We wander for distraction, but we travel for fulfillment.
— Hilaire Belloc

Date:

Attach photos, ticket stubs,
other souvenirs or sketches

Don't tell me how educated you are, tell me how much you traveled.
— Mohammed

Date:

Attach photos, ticket stubs,
other souvenirs or sketches

To be on a quest is nothing more or less than to become an asker of questions. — Sam Keen

Date:

Attach photos, ticket stubs,
other souvenirs or sketches

The traveler sees what he sees, the tourist sees what
he has come to see. — G. K. Chesterton

Date:

*Attach photos, ticket stubs,
other souvenirs or sketches*

you lose sight of things... and when you travel, everything
balances out. — Daranna Gidel

Date:

Attach photos, ticket stubs,
other souvenirs or sketches

It is only in adventure that some people succeed in knowing themselves — in finding themselves. — André Gide

Date:

Attach photos, ticket stubs,
other souvenirs or sketches

Once in a while it really hits people that they don't have to experience the world in the way they've been told. — Alan Keightley

Date:

Attach photos, ticket stubs, other souvenirs or sketches

We are all travelers in the wilderness of this world and the best we can find in our travels is an honest friend. — R.L. Stevenson

Date:

*Attach photos, ticket stubs,
other souvenirs or sketches*

Travel can be one of the most rewarding forms of introspection.
— Lawrence Durrell

Date:

Attach photos, ticket stubs,
other souvenirs or sketches

Once you have traveled, the voyage never ends. The mind can never break off from the journey. — Pat Conroy

Date:

Attach photos, ticket stubs, other souvenirs or sketches

A wise man travels to discover himself.
— James Russell Lowell

Date:

*Attach photos, ticket stubs,
other souvenirs or sketches*

See the world. It's more fantastic than any dream
made or paid for in factories. — Ray Bradbury

Attach photos, ticket stubs, other souvenirs or sketches

I would rather own little and see the world, than own the world and see little of it. — Alexander Sattler

Date:

Attach photos, ticket stubs,
other souvenirs or sketches

We travel, some of us forever, to seek other places, other lives, other souls. — Anaïs Nin

Date:

Attach photos, ticket stubs,
other souvenirs or sketches

Coming back to where you started is not the same as never leaving.
— Terry Pratchett

Date:

*Attach photos, ticket stubs,
other souvenirs or sketches*

Life is too short to wait at the baggage claim.
— Valerie Stimae

Date:

It's time to order another travel journal!

Check out our latest designs at:

MapsNotApps.co/shop

Made in the USA
Lexington, KY
17 June 2016